F Is for Frog

ABCs of Endangered Amphibians

by Lisa J. Amstutz

Consultant: Sarena Randall Gill
Community Engagement Manager
Phoenix Zoo / Arizona Center for Nature Conservation

CAPSTONE PRESS
a capstone imprint

A+ Books are published by Capstone Press,
1710 Roe Crest Drive, North Mankato, Minnesota 56003
www.mycapstone.com

Library of Congress Cataloging-in-Publication Data
Library of Congress Cataloging-in-Publication data is available on the Library of Congress website.
ISBN 978-1-4914-8033-5 (library binding)
ISBN 978-1-4914-8404-3 (eBook PDF)
Summary: Describes endangered amphibians of the world by assigning a species or amphibian-related term to each letter of the alphabet.

Editorial Credits:
Jill Kalz, editor; Bobbie Nuytten, designer; Jo Miller, media researcher;
Katy LaVigne, production specialist

Image Credits:
Alamy: blickwinkel, 22, blickwinkel/Teigier, cover (bottom right), Hombil Images, 19; Getty Images: Gallo Images/Martin Harvey, 26; Minden Pictures: Chien Lee, 14, Chris Mattison, 17, Pete Oxford, 8, 24; National Geographic Creative/Joel Sartore, 7, 9, 27, 28; Nature Picture Library: Daniel Heuclin, 10; Newscom: FLPA ImageBroker/Fabio Pupin, 25, Minden Pictures/Cyril Ruoso, 13, Minden Pictures/James Christensen, 1 (right), 29, Minden Pictures/Pete Oxford, 6, Minden Pictures/Sebastian Kennerknecht, 23; Science Source: Alvin E. Staffan, 18; Shutterstock: Anna Moskvina, 11, Dirk Ercken, 1 (left), 5, Emi, 4, Eric Isselee, 16, Joanne Weston, cover (top), 20, Quick Shot, 21, Sombra, cover (bottom left); SuperStock: age fotostock/Pablo Mendez, 12, ardea.com/Pant/Pantheon/Thomas Marent, cover (bottom middle), 15

Design Elements:
Shutterstock: Juliar Studio, Ramona Heim

Printed and bound in the USA.
009690F16

Note to Parents, Teachers, and Librarians

The E for Endangered series supports national science standards related to zoology. This book describes and illustrates amphibians. The images support early readers in understanding the text. The repetition of words and phrases helps early readers learn new words. This book also introduces early readers to subject-specific vocabulary words, which are defined in the Glossary section. Early readers may need assistance to read some words and to use the Share the Facts, Glossary, Internet Sites, Critical Thinking Using the Common Core, Read More, and Index sections of the book.

ENDANGERED!

What does it mean to be endangered?

Endangered plants and animals are at high risk of disappearing. Our planet may lose them forever because of habitat loss, hunting, or other threats. When one species goes away, the loss often hurts other species. All life on Earth is connected in some way.

All of the amphibians in this book are in trouble. They are either near threatened (at some risk), vulnerable (at more risk), or endangered. Their numbers are small. But they don't have to disappear. You can help by reading more about them and sharing what you learn with others.

Aa:
axolotl (AK-suh-lot-l)

Axolotls are salamanders that live in canals and wetlands near Mexico City, Mexico. Their name may come from two words in the Aztec language: *atl* means "water," and *xolotl* means "monster." It may also come from Xolotl, a dog-like Aztec god.

Bb:
blue-sided tree frog

Blue-sided tree frogs are nocturnal. They sleep during the day and look for food at night. They live in Costa Rica, a country in Central America. Discs on their toes stick to trees like suction cups. Blue-sided tree frogs lay their eggs on leaves overhanging ponds. The tadpoles hatch and drop into the water below.

Cc:
caecilian (seh-SILL-yen)

Caecilians look like snakes or worms. They have no legs. Some caecilian species have no eyes! Their hard, pointed heads help them burrow in moist soil. Habitat loss is the biggest threat for Mahe caecilians, Taylor's caecilians, and other caecilian species. Deforestation is destroying their rain forest homes.

RINGED CAECILIAN

Dd: defense

Amphibians protect themselves in many ways. One type of defense is bright color. Granular poison frogs look beautiful, but poisons in their skin can be deadly. Bright color warns predators to stay away. Western leopard toads defend themselves the opposite way. They blend into their surroundings.

GRANULAR POISON FROG

Ee:
elegant stubfoot toad

Elegant stubfoot toads are just over 1 inch (2.5 centimeters) long. These little toads are native to two countries in South America: Ecuador and Colombia. They live in rain forests. More than 80 percent of all elegant stubfoot toads have disappeared over the past 10 years.

Ff:
fungus

There is only one Rabb's fringe-limbed tree frog left on Earth. It lives at the Atlanta Zoo. A skin disease caused by the chytrid fungus killed the rest of its species. The disease is a danger to all amphibians. Some scientists think pollution is weakening amphibians and making them easy targets for disease.

Gg:
Goliath frog

Goliath frogs are the world's largest frogs. They live near rivers and waterfalls in western Africa. These giant amphibians are 1 foot (30 cm) long and can weigh more than 7 pounds (3.2 kilograms). Male Goliath frogs make nests in which the females lay their eggs. The nests are made of pebbles and rocks.

Hh: habitat loss

Habitat loss is a big problem for amphibians. People cut down trees for logging or to make way for farms, roads, and cities. They drain wetlands. Pollution poisons lakes and rivers. Animals can no longer live in those places. Because they cannot always move to new places, they begin to die out.

Ii:
Iberian midwife toad

Iberian midwife toads live in the European countries of Spain and Portugal. Their name comes from the way they care for their eggs. The female toad lays her eggs in a string. Then the male toad wraps them around his back legs. He keeps the eggs safe until the tadpoles are ready to hatch.

Jj:
Japanese giant salamander

Japanese giant salamanders are big! They can grow up to 5 feet (1.5 meters) long. They live in mountain streams and lakes in Japan. Japanese giant salamanders hunt fish and other small animals at night. When in danger, they release a sticky liquid that smells like peppers.

Kk:
Kadamaian stream toad

Kadamaian stream toads live in and around the mountains of Borneo, an island in Southeast Asia. These long-legged toads breed in streams. Logging has clouded many of the streams with small bits of soil called silt. The silt makes it hard for tadpoles to survive.

Ll:
Lehmann's poison frog

Bright colors tell predators to stay away from Lehmann's poison frogs. These frogs live in the rain forests of Colombia, a country in South America. The female frog lays her eggs on the ground. When the tadpoles hatch, she carries them on her back to a plant called a bromeliad. Inside the plant they can grow safely.

Mm:

Marañón (mah-rah-NYAWN) poison frog

Marañón poison frogs are polka-dotted and poisonous. They live in South America, in the mountains of Peru. They measure only about 1 inch (2.5 cm) long. These tiny frogs spend most of their lives in giant cliff-hanging bromeliads.

Nn:
newt

Newts are a type of salamander. They live in shady, moist places. They hide under rocks, in trees, or in burrows. Some species have brown or gray skin. The dull colors help them blend easily into their surroundings. Other newt species, such as the red-tailed knobby newt, have brightly colored markings that warn predators to stay away.

RED-TAILED KNOBBY NEWT

Oo:
Ozark hellbender

Ozark hellbenders live in streams in parts of Missouri and Arkansas. These shy salamanders spend most of their lives hiding under rocks. Their brown skin helps them hide easily. Ozark hellbenders come out at night to feed on crayfish and other small animals. They can reach 2 feet (61 cm) in length.

Pp:
purple frog

Purple frogs live in India near streams or ponds. These odd-looking animals spend most of their lives underground. They come out of their burrows for a few weeks each year to breed. Their feet are perfect for digging. Their pointed noses stir up termites to eat.

Qq: quantity

There are more than 7,000 known amphibians in the world. A new species is found every few days. Amphibians can be found on every continent except Antarctica. Many of them are in danger of going extinct. The biggest dangers they face are habitat loss and the deadly chytrid fungus.

BLUE-SIDED TREE FROG

Rr:
rain forest

Rain forests are hot, steamy places with lots of trees and water. Amphibians need water to grow, so rain forests make perfect homes for them. Rain forests cover only 6 percent of the earth, but they hold a lot of life. More than half of all animal species in the world live in rain forests.

Ss:
sword-tailed newt

Sword-tailed newts live in Japan. They lay their eggs in or near water. Like most amphibians, young newts hatch and live in the water. After a few weeks, they move onto land. As adults, sword-tailed newts live both on land and in water.

Tt:
tiger salamander

California tiger salamanders live only in central California. They live in burrows dug by ground squirrels and pocket gophers. They lay their eggs in shallow pools or ponds. Much of the salamanders' habitat has been turned into farms and cities.

Uu:
Urdaneta robber frog

These little frogs live in South America, in the mountain grasslands of Ecuador. Their noisy calls sound like a dog's bark. Unlike most frogs, Urdaneta robber frogs do not go through a tadpole stage. They look like tiny adults when they hatch from their eggs.

Vv: Vulnerable

Scientists use different words to describe how well species are doing. Vulnerable animals are one step away from becoming endangered. Their numbers are small and shrinking fast. Their habitats are shrinking too. They are at risk of going extinct.

Ww:
Western leopard toad

Most toads croak—but not Western leopard toads! They make a call that sounds like a deep snore. Western leopard toads live in South Africa. During spring rains, the female lays up to 25,000 eggs in jelly-like strings in the water.

Xx:
Mexican caecilian

Mexican caecilians can be found in Mexico and parts of Central America. They live mostly in forests. They burrow beneath fallen banana and coffee leaves. They feed on earthworms, snails, and insects such as crickets. Like all known caecilians, they swallow their prey whole.

Yy:
Yosemite Park toad

Yosemite Park toads live in the mountains of California. Their Latin name, *Anaxyrus canorus*, means "tuneful." Male Yosemite Park toads have a musical trill. The call helps them attract a mate. Female toads lay their eggs in pools left by melted snow. After hatching, the tadpoles live there for up to 60 days. Then they grow legs and move onto land.

Zz:
zoo

Zoos are fun places to see animals. But they're also important for saving at-risk animals. Many zoos breed endangered animals, including amphibians. They hope to return some of the young animals to the wild one day. The La Loma tree frog and Limosa harlequin frog are two species that depend on zoos for their survival.

LIMOSA HARLEQUIN FROG

SHARE THE FACTS

- Nearly one-third of the 6,260 species of amphibians that have been studied are now endangered.

- Amphibians are easily affected by change. Slight changes in temperature or moisture can hurt their life cycles in big ways.

- The critically endangered Chinese giant salamander is the largest amphibian on Earth.

- The Rabb's fringe-limbed tree frog can spread its limbs and large webbed feet to glide to the ground from heights of up to 30 feet (9 m).

- Unlike most salamanders, the axolotl never really grows up. After hatching, it lives in the water its whole life.

- Roasted axolotl is a delicacy in Mexico.

- The Ozark hellbender is North America's largest salamander.

- Newts usually have dry, rough skin. A salamander's skin is smooth and moist.

- If a newt or axolotl loses its leg or tail, it can grow a new one.

- You can help save amphibians! FrogWatch USA volunteers collect information on frogs and toads in their area. The information helps scientists decide how to protect them. Visit www.aza.org/ become-a-frogwatch-volunteer/ for more information.

GLOSSARY

amphibian—an animal with a backbone that relies on the environment to control its body temperature; most amphibians live in water when young and can live on land as adults

breed—to help produce young

bromeliad (broh-MEE-lee-ad)—a tropical plant with long, stiff leaves

deforestation—cutting down trees until a forest is destroyed

endangered—at risk of disappearing forever

extinct—when a species no longer exists on Earth

habitat—a place where an animal can find its food, water, shelter, and space to live

near threatened—could become endangered in the near future

pollution—materials that hurt Earth's water, air, and land

predator—an animal that hunts and eats other animals

protect—to save from danger

species—a group of plants or animals that share common traits

tadpole—the stage of a frog's or toad's growth between the egg and adult stages

vulnerable—at high risk of becoming endangered

INTERNET SITES

FactHound offers a safe, fun way to find Internet sites related to this book. All of the sites on FactHound have been researched by our staff.

Here's all you do:

Visit *www.facthound.com*

Type in this code: 9781491480335

 Check out projects, games and lots more at
www.capstonekids.com

CRITICAL THINKING USING THE COMMON CORE

1. Name three reasons why an amphibian species may become endangered. (Key Ideas and Details)

2. Explain how bright skin color may protect an amphibian from predators. (Craft and Structure)

3. Why are rain forests the perfect homes for amphibians? (Key Ideas and Details)

READ MORE

Berger, Melvin, and Glenda. *Amphibians*. Scholastic True or False. New York: Scholastic, 2011.

Orr, Tamra B. *Poison Dart Frog*. Exploring Our Rainforests. Ann Arbor, Mich.: Cherry Lake Publishing, 2014.

Pope, Kristen. *Salamanders*. Mankato, Minn.: Child's World, 2015.

Ransom, Candice. *Endangered and Extinct Amphibians*. Animals in Danger. Minneapolis: Lerner Publications Company, 2014.

INDEX